LEVEL 3

Nelson Mandela

Barbara Kramer

NATIONAL GEOGRAPHIC

Washington, D.C.

For Cindy and Ted —B. K.

The publisher and author gratefully acknowledge the expert review
of this book by the Nelson Mandela Foundation.

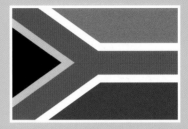

Paperback ISBN: 978-1-4263-1763-7
Reinforced Library Binding ISBN: 978-1-4263-1764-4

Book design by YAY! Design

Cover, Trevor Samson/AFP/Getty Images; 1, David Forman/Corbis; 2, Globe Turner/Shutterstock; 5, Denis Farrell/AP Images; 6, courtesy of Charles van Onselen/NMF; 7 (UP), David Turnley/Corbis; 7 (LO), Zen Icknow/Corbis; 9, Felix Dlangamandla/Foto24/ Gallo Images/Alamy Live News/Alamy; 10-11, Susan Winters Cook/Getty Images; 12, Carl de Souza/AFP/Getty Images; 13, Chip Somodevilla/Getty Images; 15 (UP), PKA Gaeshwe/Black Star; 15 (LO), courtesy of the Stengile family/NMF; 16 (UP), Fox Photos/Getty Images; 16 (LO), Eric Isselee/Shutterstock; 17 (UP), Fox Photos/Hulton Archive Creative/Getty Images; 17 (CTR), Roger De La Harpe/ Gallo Images/Corbis; 17 (LO), Alain Nogues/Sygma/Corbis; 18-19, courtesy of University of Fort Hare; 20, Amadou Keita/Demotix/ Corbis; 21, Markus Schreiber/AP Images; 23, Jurgen Schadeberg/Hulton Archive/Getty Images; 25, Jurgen Schadeberg/Getty Images; 26, Keystone-France/Gamma-Keystone via Getty Images; 27, OFF/AFP/Getty Images; 29, Mary Benson/Felicity Brian Literary Agency/Sygma/Corbis; 30, Frank Micelotta/Getty Images; 32 (UP), Erik S. Lesser/AP Images; 32 (CTR), API/Gamma-Rapho via Getty Images; 32 (LO), Oryx Media Archive/Gallo Images/Getty Images; 32 (BACKGROUND), Tatyana Alexandrova/Shutterstock; 33 (UPLE), Steve Pyke/Contour by Getty Images; 33 (UPRT), courtesy of the National Archives of South Africa; 33 (CTR LE), Mark Wilson/AP Images; 33 (CTR RT), Alexander Gardner/Library of Congress Prints & Photographs Division; 33 (LO), Dai Kurokawa/epa/Corbis; 34-35, Gideon Mendel/Corbis; 37, Alexander Joe/AFP/Getty Images; 37 (INSET), Tom Stoddart Archive/Reportage/Getty Images; 38, Andrew Ingram/POOL/AP Images; 39, Jon Eeg/AP Images; 40 (UP), Javier Soriano/AFP/Getty Images; 40 (LO), Stephen Jaffe/POOL/ AP Images; 41 (UP), Walter Dhladhla/AFP/Getty Images; 41 (LO), Oryx Media Archive/Gallo Images/Getty Images; 43, Mike Hutchings/Reuters/Corbis; 44 (UP), Gaeshwe/Black Star; 44 (CTR), Chip Somodevilla/Getty Images; 44 (LO), API/Gamma-Rapho via Getty Images; 45 (UP), courtesy of the Mandela Foundation; 45 (CTR LE), Alexander Joe/AFP/Getty Images; 45 (CTR RT), Media24/Gallo Images/Getty Images; 45 (LO), Javier Soriano/AFP/Getty Images; 46 (UP), Jurgen Schadeberg/Hulton Archive/Getty Images; 46 (CTR LE), michaeljung/Shutterstock; 46 (CTR RT), Jurgen Schadeberg/Getty Images; 46 (LOLE), Lisa S./Shutterstock; 46 (LORT), Jeff Kowalsky/AFP/Getty Images; 47 (UPLE), Joey Foley/FilmMagic/Getty Images; 47 (UPRT), Walter Dhladhla/AFP/Getty Images; 47 (CTR LE), Martin Cleaver/AP Images; 47 (CTR RT), David Turnley/Corbis; 47 (LOLE), Keystone-France/Gamma-Keystone via Getty Images; 47 (LORT), George F. Mobley/National Geographic Creative; header (THROUGHOUT), balabolka/Shutterstock; vocab (THROUGH-OUT), Robert Biedermann/Shutterstock

National Geographic supports K–12 educators with ELA Common Core Resources.
Visit natgeoed.org/commoncore for more information.

Printed in the United States of America
14/WOR/1

Table of Contents

Who Was Nelson Mandela?. 4

The Son of a Chief. 8

A New Home 10

Changes. 12

Learning to Lead. 14

In His Time 16

Student Protest. 18

Runaway 20

New Ideas 22

A Long Trial 26

A New Direction 28

Life in Prison 30

8 Cool Facts About Mandela 32

Free Mandela!. 34

Talking About Peace 36

A New Life 40

Be a Quiz Whiz! 44

Glossary. 46

Index. 48

Who Was Nelson Mandela?

What if you lived in a country where you were judged by the color of your skin? If almost everyone you knew was black, but the government was controlled by a few white people.

The government told you where to live and where you could go to school. If they wanted the land you lived on, they could take it. White people made all the laws. They also decided who would rule the country. That was the way it was in South Africa, where Nelson Mandela lived.

Mandela believed all people should be treated the same. The color of their skin should not matter. He became a fighter for equal rights. It was a hard battle. He spent many years in prison because of his beliefs, but he did not quit. His fight against racism (RACE-is-um) made him a hero to people all around the world.

Words to Know

EQUAL RIGHTS: Treating all people the same

RACISM: Treating people poorly because of their race

In His Own Words

"Real leaders must be ready to sacrifice all for the freedom of their people."

CITY OF PORT ELIZABETH
NOTICE
FOR WHITE PERSONS ONLY.
BY ORDER.

STAD PORT ELIZABETH
KENNISGEWING
SLEGS VIR BLANKES.
OP LAS.

IDOLOPHU YASEBHAYI
ISAZISO
ABANTU ABA - MHLOPE
BODWA.
NGOMYALELO.

Apartheid

In South Africa, there were laws that kept black and white people apart. Those laws were called apartheid (uh-PAR-tide). Black Africans had to live in their own section of town. They had their own schools and hospitals that were not as nice as those for white people. It was a crime for them to eat in restaurants for white people or to ride "white only" buses.

ANTI-APARTHEID
MOVEMENT SAYS
STOP
APARTHEID
REPRESSION
AAM, 13 Mandela Street, London NW1 0DW. Tel: 01 387 7966

ANTI-APARTHEID
MOVEMENT CALLS
FOR A UNITED
NON-RACIAL
DEMOCRATIC
SOUTH AFRICA
AAM, 13 Mandela Street, London NW1 0DW. Tel: 01 387 7966

ANTI-APARTHEID
MOVEMENT SAYS
SOLIDARITY
WITH
ANC
AAM, 13 Mandela Street, London NW1 0DW. Tel: 01 387 7966

SMASH
APARTHEID

The Son of a Chief

Mandela was born in the South African village of Mvezo (muh–VAY-zoh) on July 18, 1918. His father named him Rolihlahla (ho-lee-LHA-lha), which means "troublemaker."

Words to Know

TRIBE: A group of people who share the same language and culture

NAMIBIA

BOTSWANA

MOZAMBIQUE

SWAZILAND

SOUTH AFRICA

LESOTHO

Atlantic Ocean

Mvezo• •Qunu

Indian Ocean

A hut like the one Mandela was born in

His father was a chief of the Thembu (TEM-boo) tribe. One day when Mandela was very young, his father disagreed with a white judge in the village. The angry judge removed Mandela's father from his position as chief. He also took the family's land. Mandela's mother moved her family to a farm in the nearby village of Qunu (KOO-noo).

That's a Fact! In the culture of the Thembu people, men could have more than one wife at the same time. Mandela's father had four wives and thirteen children.

A New Home

South African men returning home to their village of Qunu

The family lived in three huts. One was for sleeping, one for cooking, and one for storage. The huts had mud walls, dirt floors, and grass roofs. Everyone had work to do. Mandela began herding goats and sheep when he was only five years old.

That's a Fact! Mandela sometimes wore a blanket wrapped around one shoulder and pinned at the waist.

When he was seven, Mandela became the first person in his family to attend school. On the first day, the teacher gave the students English names. She said he would be called Nelson.

Changes

In 1930, Mandela's father died. He had been a friend to the king of the Thembu people. After his death, the king invited 12-year-old Mandela to live with him. Mandela's mother did not want to let her son go. But she knew the king could give him a good life.

This banner hangs in the Great Place, where Mandela, also called "Madiba," lived with the king.

The Great Place had many buildings.

Mandela was sad as he left Qunu. He wondered if he would ever see his village or his family again. When he got to the village of Mqhekezweni (mm-khe-KHE-zweh-nee), Mandela could not believe his eyes. The king had the grandest home he had ever seen. It included two houses and seven huts. It was known as the Great Place.

Learning to Lead

Mandela learned his first lessons about being a good leader from the king. In tribal meetings, the king gave everyone a chance to talk. He listened carefully to what each person said.

The chiefs who visited the Great Place taught Mandela about the history of the tribe. They told him stories about African heroes.

Mandela's education continued at a one-room school next door to the Great Place until he was 15. Then he went to the Clarkebury Boarding Institute about 60 miles away. In 1937, he moved to Healdtown to attend college.

Mandela as a young man

Healdtown College class picture, 1938

In His Time

In the 1920s, when Nelson Mandela was a child, life in South Africa was very different from how it is now.

School

Many black children did not attend school at all. Most who did went to one-room schools in their villages. The schools were run by people who traveled to South Africa to do work for their church.

Home Life

A few wealthy families in Mandela's village were able to buy sugar, tea, and coffee, but most people ate only what they grew. That included beans, pumpkins, and corn. They drank milk from cows and goats.

Transportation

Many white people drove cars, but Mandela and most others in his village walked.

Toys and Free Time

Children in Mandela's village made their own toys using clay and sticks. They played games such as hide-and-seek and tag. The boys enjoyed stick fighting.

History

South Africa was ruled by white European settlers. They owned much of the land and made all the laws.

Student Protest

Mandela started classes at Fort Hare University when he was 20 years old. He worked hard at his studies, but he had fun too. He was on the cross-country running team. He also played soccer.

Fort Hare University

In his second year, Mandela was elected to serve on the student council. There were about 150 students, but only 25 of them voted. The others were upset about the bad food served in the cafeteria. They protested by not voting.

Mandela wanted to support the other students. He said he would not serve on the student council. The principal said Mandela needed to take his place on the student council or leave the school. Mandela left.

Words to Know

ELECTED: Chosen for a position or office by the act of voting

PROTEST: To speak or act in a way that shows you do not agree with something

 Runaway

Back at the Great Place, Mandela learned the king was arranging a marriage for him. Mandela was not ready to get married. So he ran away to Johannesburg.

An Arranged Marriage

In an arranged marriage, families decide who their children should marry. Often the marriage is used to bring two families together. Sometimes one family gives the other family money or other gifts as part of the agreement.

An arranged marriage ceremony in Africa

It was a large, modern city, but Mandela had to live in a section for black people only. The homes in that area were small. They had no electricity or running water.

The only work many black men could find was in the gold and diamond mines in the area. The white owners were getting rich from the mines. But the black miners worked long hours for little pay.

Mandela's first home in Johannesburg

New Ideas

Mandela got a job working as a clerk in the law office of a white lawyer. He wanted to become a lawyer, and this was the first step. He also took classes to finish college.

He met many people in Johannesburg. Some of them were members of the African National Congress (ANC), a group that was working for equal rights for black Africans. Mandela joined them in 1944.

That same year, he married Evelyn Mase, the cousin of one of his best friends. They had two sons and two daughters. Sadly, one daughter died as a baby.

Words to Know

LAWYER: A person whose job is to help people with things related to the law

That's a Fact! Black Africans who were at least 16 years old had to carry a passbook. It showed who they were and where they lived.

An ANC rally in Johannesburg for equal pay and voting rights

By the 1950s, Mandela had become a leader in the ANC. He helped organize marches and strikes. He was also busy with work. In 1952, he and his friend Oliver Tambo set up the first black law office in South Africa.

Mandela left early in the morning for work. In the evenings, he had ANC meetings. Many times, he did not get home until late at night. His children were already sleeping. His oldest son asked why his father was not there more. Mandela tried to explain. He was working to make life better for millions of black Africans.

Words to Know

STRIKE: A kind of protest in which a group of people stop work until they are treated fairly

Mandela in his law office

That's a Fact!

Mandela started law school but had to stop. After passing a written test, he was allowed to practice law.

A Long Trial

Mandela arrives by bus for a day at the trial.

In 1956, Mandela was arrested along with 155 other activists. They were charged with treason (TREE-zon), or trying to overthrow the government. The trial lasted four years.

Mandela's wife Evelyn did not agree with his work with the ANC. One day during the trial, she took their children and left. Their marriage was over.

The trial was still going on when he met Winnie Madikizela (ma-dee-kee-ZAY-lah). They were married in 1958 and had two daughters.

That's a Fact!

Winnie and Mandela shared many of the same ideas. She also joined the ANC.

A New Direction

The trial finally ended in 1961. Mandela and those tried with him were found not guilty. After the trial, Mandela went into hiding. The government was watching him closely. It was too dangerous for him to do his work with the ANC out in the open. He moved often so the police would not find him. He met with other ANC members in secret.

Mandela said peaceful protests were not working. It was time to take stronger action. He helped create a military branch of the ANC and became its leader.

Mandela traveled to other countries to get their help. He also trained to become a soldier.

Mandela visited London while traveling to other countries to get support.

Soon after Mandela returned to South Africa, he was arrested. This time, he was found guilty of leaving the country without a passport and of leading a strike. He was sentenced to five years in prison.

While he was serving his sentence, he was put on trial again. This time he was charged with trying to overthrow the

government. On June 11, 1964, he was sentenced to spend the rest of his life in prison. Mandela was 45 years old.

He was sent to the Robben (RAH–bin) Island Prison off the coast of Cape Town. His cell was small. When he lay down to sleep, his head touched one wall and his feet touched the other. His bed was a thin mat on the floor. He was given a bucket to use as a toilet.

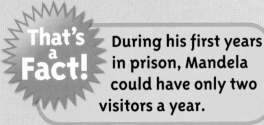

That's a Fact! During his first years in prison, Mandela could have only two visitors a year.

8 Cool Facts About Mandela

1

LONG WALK TO FREEDOM

Kind regards and
Best Wishes to~
Peabo Bryson

NMandela
23

In prison, Mandela secretly wrote a book about his fight for equal rights. That book, *Long Walk to Freedom*, was published in 1994.

2

Mandela enjoyed boxing for exercise.

3

Mandela was the 466th prisoner at Robben Island in 1964. His prison number 466/64 became a sign of freedom.

4

To keep fit while he was in prison, Mandela ran in place for 45 minutes. Then he did 200 sit-ups and 100 push-ups.

5

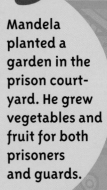

Mandela planted a garden in the prison court-yard. He grew vegetables and fruit for both prisoners and guards.

6

Mandela has received more than 1,000 awards. More than 45 schools have been named after him.

7

One leader Mandela admired was Abraham Lincoln. Mandela learned about him in school.

8

Nelson Mandela International Day is celebrated every year on his birthday, July 18.

Free Mandela!

In prison, Mandela was a leader. He used peaceful protests to help the prisoners get better food. They also got books so they could study. Other prisoners, and even some of the white guards, admired Mandela. He was brave and never gave up hope.

That's a Fact! In 1988, 72,000 people attended a concert to celebrate Mandela's 70th birthday. Millions more watched at home.

Outside the prison, he was not forgotten. In the 1980s, the ANC started a "Free Mandela" campaign. "Free Mandela" posters went up around the world. Students marched to show their support. Other governments put pressure on South Africa. They would not buy products made in South Africa or play sports against the country's teams.

A Nelson Mandela Freedom Festival in London in 1986

Words to Know

CAMPAIGN: A group of activities planned to get a certain result

In 1982, after 18 years at Robben Island, Mandela was moved to a different prison. On the streets, fighting between the police and protesters was getting worse. Mandela knew it was time for a change. While still in prison, he met with people from the South African government. They talked about peace and equal rights.

In 1989, F.W. de Klerk became the new president of South Africa. He also wanted peace. On February 11, 1990, he released Mandela from prison. Mandela was 71 years old and had spent 27 years of his life in prison.

Thousands cheered as Mandela walked away from prison with Winnie by his side.

In His Own Words

"My life was beginning anew. My ten thousand days of imprisonment were at last over."

There was still a lot of work to do.
Mandela and President de Klerk had
many meetings to talk about the future of
South Africa. They did not always agree,
but they worked together to end apartheid.
They also worked to create a free country,
where people of all races could vote.

On April 27, 1994, black Africans in South Africa were able to vote for the first time. They elected Mandela. He became the first black president of South Africa. He was 75 years old.

As president, he talked about forgiveness. The country had been divided. Now it was time for people of all races to work together.

An Award for Peace

In 1993, Mandela and F. W. de Klerk were awarded the Nobel Peace Prize. It is an international award, the highest honor given to someone who has worked for peace.

A New Life

During Mandela's many years in prison, he and Winnie had both changed. They ended their marriage in 1996. Two years later on his 80th birthday, Mandela married Graca Machel (GRA-sah Ma-SHELL).

Mandela served one five-year term as president. Then he stepped down. He said it was time for a younger person to lead. In 1999, he began spending most of his time at his house in Johannesburg.

1918
Born at Mvezo,
South Africa, on July 18

1930
His father
dies

1941
Runs away to
Johannesburg

Mandela and his wife Graca

Mandela being sworn in as president in 1994

President Mandela shows U.S. President Clinton his jail cell.

Thabo Mbeki replaced Mandela as president.

1944

Joins the ANC and marries Evelyn Mase

1952

Opens the first black law firm in South Africa

1958

Marries Winnie Madikizela

Mandela also had a country home in Qunu, the village where he lived as a child. He listened to music, spent time with family, and enjoyed watching the sun set. They were all things he had not been able to do for the many years when he was in prison. He died on December 5, 2013, when he was 95 years old.

It was a sad day for people around the world as they remembered the man who had inspired them. He taught us about courage as he fought bravely for equal rights. He showed us hope, never giving up even when almost everything was taken from him.

1964
Sentenced to life in prison

1990
Released from prison

1994
Elected president of South Africa

He taught us to forgive and showed us how to live in peace. He united a nation and changed the world, making it a better place for everyone.

1998	1999	2013
Marries Graca Machel	Steps down as president	Dies on December 5

Be a Quiz Whiz!

See how many questions you can get right! Answers are at the bottom of page 45.

Mandela was given the name Nelson by:
A. His parents
B. His first teacher
C. The king of the Thembu tribe
D. A white judge

After his father died, Mandela went to live at:
A. The Palace
B. The Kingdom
C. The Great Place
D. Johannesburg

When he was 20, Mandela:
A. Moved to Johannesburg
B. Started playing sports
C. Began classes at Fort Hare University
D. Got a job at a law office

4

Nelson Mandela International Day is celebrated on:
A. January 15
B. May 3
C. July 18
D. September 21

5

In 1964, Mandela was found guilty of trying to overthrow the government and sentenced to:
A. 4 years in prison
B. 35 years of hard labor
C. 50 years in prison
D. Life in prison

6

In 1990, Mandela was released after _____ years in prison.
A. 18
B. 27
C. 35
D. 41

Laws in South Africa that kept black and white people apart were known as:
A. Apartheid
B. Treason
C. Tribal laws
D. Equal rights

7

Answers: 1) B, 2) C, 3) C, 4) C, 5) D, 6) B, 7) A

Glossary

ACTIVIST: A person who works to make changes

EQUAL RIGHTS: Treating all people the same

LAWYER: A person whose job is to help people with things related to the law

SENTENCED: To be told in a court of law what the punishment for a crime will be

STRIKE: A kind of protest in which a group of people stop work until they are treated fairly

CAMPAIGN: A group of activities planned to get a certain result

ELECTED: Chosen for a position or office by the act of voting

PROTEST: To speak or act in a way that shows you do not agree with something

RACISM: Treating people poorly because of their race

TREASON: The crime of trying to overthrow, or take over, a country's government

TRIBE: A group of people who share the same language and culture

Index

Bold page numbers indicate illustrations.

A
Activists 26, 27, 46
African National Congress (ANC) 22, 24, 27, 28, 35
Apartheid 7, 38
Arranged marriages 20, **20**

C
Campaigns 35, 47
Clinton, Bill **40–41**

D
De Klerk, F. W. 36, 38, **38, 39**
Diamond mines 21

E
Equal rights 6, 22, 32, 36, 42, 46

F
Fort Hare University, South Africa 18, **18–19**
"Free Mandela" campaign 35

G
Goats 10, 16, **16**
Gold mines 21
The Great Place, Mqhekezweni, South Africa **12**, 13, **13**, 14, 20, **44**

H
Healdtown College, Healdtown, South

Africa 14, **14–15**
Huts **9**, 10, 13

J
Johannesburg, South Africa 20–21, **21**, 22, **23**, 40

L
Lincoln, Abraham 33, **33**
Long Walk to Freedom (Mandela) 32, **32**

M
Mandela, Evelyn Mase 22, 27, 41
Mandela, Graca Machel 40, **40–41**, 43
Mandela, Nelson
arrests and trials 26–27, 28, 30–31
awards 33, 39, **39**
birthday 8, 33, 34, 40
childhood 9–14, 16–17
death 42, 43
education 11, 14, 18, 22, 25
imprisonment 30–31, 32, 33, 34, 36
jail cell **30**, 31, **40–41**
law practice 24, 25, 41
marriages 22, 27, 40, 43
as president 39, 40, **41**, 42, 43
release from prison 36, 42
work with ANC 22, 24, 27, 28
Mandela, Winnie Madikizela 27, **27, 37**, 40, 41

Mbeki, Thabo **41**
Mvezo, South Africa 8, 40

N
Nelson Mandela International Day 33, 45
Nobel Peace Prize 39, **39**

P
Protests and rallies **7**, 19, **22–23**, 28, 34, **46**, 47, **47**

Q
Qunu, South Africa 9, **10–11**, 13, 42

R
Racism 6, 47
Robben Island, South Africa 31, **32**, 36
Rolihlahla ("troublemaker") 8

S
Strikes 24, 30, 46

T
Tambo, Oliver 24
Thembu tribe 9, 12
Treason 26, 27, 47

V
Voting rights 23, 38